FLAGS
DO
CRY

A H Faughsgate

Freedom to differ is not limited to things that do not matter much. That would be a mere shadow of freedom. The test of its substance is the right to differ as to things that touch the heart of the existing order. If there is any fixed star in our constitutional constellation it is that no official, high or petty, can prescribe what shall be orthodox in politics, nationalism, religion or other matters of opinion.

Inspired by a story, told by GUY LANGSTON....

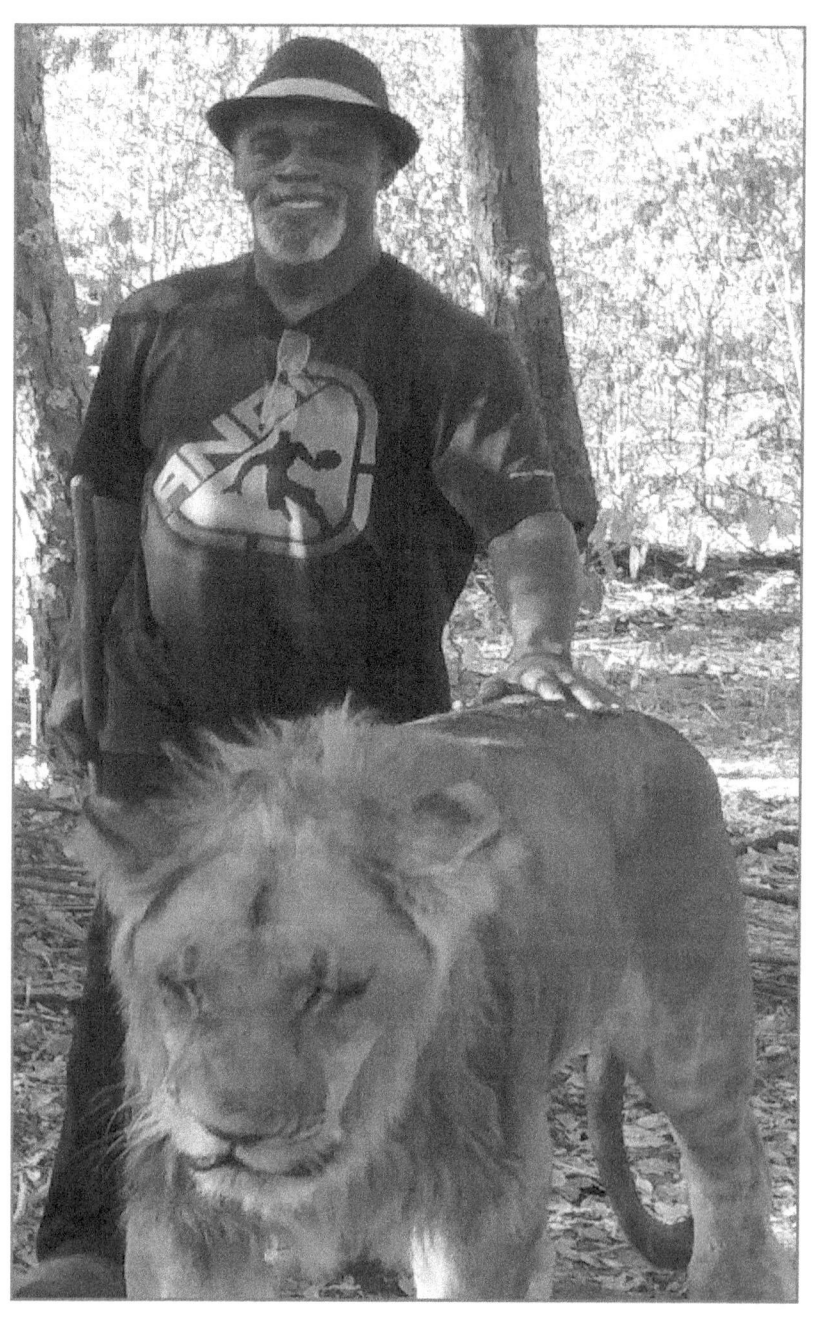

Oh, Lord!
Why do my
children love
themselves so, and
each other naught?

ACCENSSION

A Star is Born

I know, you what I am, but you do not know who I am.

I started off as less than an inkling of an idea in the the hearts of some brave freedom fighters.

Before I was ever commissioned, my essence with within.

My very existence is recognized, worldwide... to give a feeling freedom and ability to all.

But, why was I even created...

The stripes represent the original 13 Colonies and the stars represent the 50 states of the Union. The colors of the flag are symbolic as well; red symbolizes hardiness and valor, white symbolizes purity and innocence, and blue represents vigilance, perseverance and justice.

I am utilized to display nationalism, as well as the rebel in the hearts of our first founders, as they searched relentlessly for freedom of religion and common wealth. I am a symbol for the story of America, her struggle, battles and triumphs.

I am you, and you...you are me. We represent each other.

I also represent dignity, and the absolute freedoms, that express being an American.

From 1777, to the present, mine eyes have witness, not only a birth of a nation, but the the nation's ability to hoist itself into the most elite circles in the world.

I've witnessed civil development, civility demised, and Civil War!
My metamorphosis, over time also mirrors our set backs and

accomplishments, that we have endured together.
So, now you ask,
"Why I cry?"
I stand for unity, peace and harmony under the eyes of God, so I challenge you to ask yourself,
"Do I commit to ideal of Ol' Glory?"

MERIT

The Efforts of the Many

My citizens, come from all over the world, and as I am, a "Melting Pot", due to my diversity, I hold apprehension, as my diversity delivers more divide than duality.

As no one human race can claim America for themselves, I recognize, that the civil unrest within, is atrocious!

My beautiful white children, I beg of you to release the animosity and anger and bitterness and become the true and the truth of being an American beacon.

My beautiful black children, you are home, and very humble, sincere and truthful apology is deserved by you all. Quietly I have observed the heinous and despicable and morbid barely unspeakable violations, you have endured at the hands of your own fellow countrymen. I allow my tears to flow for you. Please stay strong and true to your truth...thus, instilling and maintaining rawness, ore, the core value, of a true American.

My beautiful foreign children, born here, and abroad...if you will love me, I will love you, as well. Your longing to be, to express, to want to and experience, makes you the epitome of the spirit that brought the fore-fathers here so many years ago. You represent what it is to be an American as well.

My children, can you truthfully admit to yourself that you truly love yourself with **any amount of hate in your heart**?

EXISTENTIAL

MY CHILDREN

All mine
All colors
All walks
All races
All languages
All facets
All levels
All religions
All faiths
All humans
All Americans

IN MY NAME

Recognized internationally as a symbol of strength, quality and competency, we are the bar.   We set the standard of quality, for the best.

As a nation that has experienced phenomenal growth, I do in my heart of hearts believe, we must realize...**THE ENTIRE WORLD IS WHATCHING US!**

Also, as a little brother nation with so much expansion and hearth, it will be easy for us to be a target.

When you're up, only one way to go!

And that is...**DOWN!**
We could very well be the cause of our own demise!
Individual feelings and lines of difference must be eliminated. Providers of salacious, hateful, harmful and discriminatory educations, should be silenced, avoided and simply ignored, as they only bring self-destruction and chaos and repugnant, vile ugliness that takes away from the moral fibers and community effort of the collective!

As an individual, become apart of something not only bigger than you, but...something that allows comradery, fellowship and community with all of your fellow Americans.
DO THIS... IN MY NAME, OL' GLORY!

REPROCITY

STAND ON ME

STAND...
by me,
for me,
with me,
along me...
on me!

Your stand is your stand, your
have that right as an American.
Some stand with a fist, some with
their heart...others stand with a
knee!

Change In America

"The only constant in life, is change!"

-Heraclitus

This must be a seriously conscious effort, as we not only jeopardize the core values of the land that our fore-fathers' have left us, but we may very well robbing our children of the future with liberties that we have always held so near and dear.

The collective, us...The USA, the greatest country in the world can heal herself, if we wanted to.

We have to want to...therefore, I cry.

No human is perfect, and no one should think so, but degradation and demoralization is not any means acquire any type of upper-hand.

We are descendants of people who were searchers of the liberties that was denied them in their own home country...and, yes, that same blood and spirit is still prevalent today...right now, in each of us...us...U.S.!

If change is going to happen anyway, why shan't we guide change in the defection in which, we would like for it to favor.

"No one won the last war, and no one will win the next war!"
-Eleanor Roosevelt

Our energy, spirit and integrity is on the line.   As the world watch, we can become the largest WWE Royal Rumble event ever.

INTERPRETATION

NOW OR NEVER

TO RECKON
TO OPEN
TO SEE
TO FEEL
TO EMPATHIZE
TO GROW
TO SHARE
TO LIVE
TO CHANGE
TO CHOOSE
WE TAKE TODAY

As an American, you must be
compassionate, caring and constant,
with the integrity of our
own...mistakes have been made, but

we choose today to take
us...us...US...BACK!

CULTURE

244 Years of Tears

From Francis Hopkinson, to
Betty Ross, to Francis Scott Key, to
William Diver, to Paul Revere, to
Harriet Tubman, to Josiah Henson,
to Mike Tyson to Colin Kaepernick,
you are all my children, I love you
all and the individual ways you
show your patronage.

Our diversity has made us the
great nation we've known to
become, so in the most infamous
words of Rodney King,

"Can we all just get along?"

Please, I beg of you, my
children, please don't make me
have to endure another 244 years of

tears, as progress is supposed to move all forward, and unity with genuine peace for all is forward!

ASHAMED

We all have history, here is mine, my growth and changes...

1776	January 1 — The Grand Union flag (Continental Colors) is displayed on Prospect Hill. It has 13 alternate red and white stripes and the British Union Jack in the upper left-hand corner (the canton).
1776	May — Betsy Ross reports that she sewed the first American flag
1777	Another 13-star flag, in the 3-2-3-2-3 pattern.

1777?	Cowpens Flag. According to some sources, this flag was first used in 1777. It was used by the Third Maryland Regiment. There was no official pattern for how the stars were to be arranged. The flag was carried at the Battle of Cowpens, which took place on January 17, 1781, in South Carolina. The actual flag from that battle hangs in the Maryland State House.
1777	Brandywine Flag.
1777	June 14 — Continental Congress adopts the following: *Resolved: that the flag of the United States be thirteen stripes, alternate red and white; that the union be thirteen stars, white in a blue field, representing a new constellation.* Stars represent **Delaware (December 7, 1787), Pennsylvania (December 12, 1787), New Jersey (December 18, 1787), Georgia (January**

	2, 1788), Connecticut (January 9, 1788), Massachusetts (February 6, 1788), Maryland (April 28, 1788), South Carolina (May 23, 1788), New Hampshire (June 21, 1788), Virginia (June 25, 1788), New York (July 26, 1788), North Carolina (November 21, 1789), and Rhode Island (May 29, 1790)
1779	John Paul Jones Flag, also called the Serapis Flag.
1781?	The Guilford Flag.
1787	Captain Robert Gray carries the flag around the world on his sailing vessel (around the tip of South America, to China, and beyond). He discovered a great river and named it after his boat *The Columbia.* His discovery was the basis of America's claim to the Oregon Territory.
1795	Flag with 15 stars and 15 stripes **Vermont**

	(March 4, 1791), Kentucky (June 1, 1792)
1803	Indian Peace Flag.
1814	September 14 — Francis Scott Key writes "The Star-Spangled Banner." It officially becomes the national anthem in 1931.
1814	Easton Flag.
1818	Flag with 20 stars and 13 stripes (it remains at 13 hereafter) **Tennessee (June 1, 1796), Ohio (March 1, 1803), Louisiana (April 30, 1812), Indiana (December 11, 1816), Mississippi (December 10, 1817)**
1819	Flag with 21 stars **Illinois**

	(December 3, 1818)
1820	Flag with 23 stars **Alabama (December 14, 1819), Maine (March 15, 1820)** first flag on Pikes Peak
c. 1820-30	Bennington Flag. According to some accounts, this flag was flown at the Battle of Bennington. It is sometimes called the Fillmore Flag. The story goes that Nathaniel Fillmore took this flag home from the battlefield, and the flag was passed down through generations of Fillmores, including Millard, and today it can be seen at Vermont's Bennington Museum. Most experts doubt

	this story and date the flag to about 1820-30.
1822	Flag with 24 stars **Missouri (August 10, 1821)**
1836	Flag with 25 stars **Arkansas (June 15, 1836)**
1837	Flag with 26 stars **Michigan (Jan 26, 1837)**
1837	Great Star Flag.
1845	Flag with 27 stars **Florida (March 3, 1845)**

1846	Flag with 28 stars **Texas** (December 29, 1845)
1847	Flag with 29 stars **Iowa** (December 28, 1846)
1847	29 Star Flag.
1848	Flag with 30 stars **Wisconsin** (May 29, 1848)
1851	Flag with 31 stars **California** (September 9, 1850)
1858	Flag with 32 stars **Minnesota**

	(May 11, 1858)
1859	Flag with 33 stars **Oregon (February 14, 1859)**
1861	Flag with 34 stars; **Kansas (January 29, 1861)** Note: Even after the South seceded from the Union, President Lincoln would not allow any stars to be removed from the flag. • first Confederate Flag (Stars and Bars) adopted in Montgomery, Alabama
1861	Fort Sumter Flag.
1863	

	Flag with 35 stars **West Virginia (June 20, 1863)**
1865	
	Flag with 36 stars **Nevada (October 31, 1864)**
1867	
	Flag with 37 stars **Nebraska (March 1, 1867)**
1869	
	First flag on a postage stamp
1876	
	Centennial Flag.
1877	
	Flag with 38 stars **Colorado (August 1, 1876)**

1877	38 Star Flag.
1889	Flag with 39 stars that never was! Flag manufacturers believed that the two Dakotas would be admitted as one state and so manufactured this flag, some of which still exist. It was never an official flag.
1890	Flag with 43 stars **North Dakota (November 2, 1889), South Dakota (November 2, 1889), Montana (November 8, 1889), Washington (November 11, 1889), Idaho (July 3, 1890)**
1891	Flag with 44 stars **Wyoming**

	(July 10, 1890)
1892	"Pledge of Allegiance" first published in a magazine called "The Youth's Companion," written by Francis Bellamy.
1896	Flag with 45 stars **Utah (January 4, 1896)**
1897	Adoption of State Flag Desecration Statutes — By the late 1800's an organized flag protection movement was born in reaction to perceived commercial and political misuse of the flag. After supporters failed to obtain federal legislation, Illinois, Pennsylvania, and South Dakota became the first States to adopt flag desecration statutes. By 1932, all of the States had

adopted flag desecration laws.

In general, these State laws outlawed: (i) placing any kind of marking on the flag, whether for commercial, political, or other purposes; (ii) using the flag in any form of advertising; and (iii) publicly mutilating, trampling, defacing, defiling, defying or casting contempt, either by words or by act, upon the flag. Under the model flag desecration law, the term "flag" was defined to include any flag, standard, ensign, or color, or any representation of such made of any substance whatsoever and of any size that evidently purported to be said flag or a picture or representation thereof, upon which shall be shown the

	colors, the stars and stripes in any number, or by which the person seeing the same without deliberation may believe the same to represent the flag of the U.S.
1907	Halter v. Nebraska (205 U.S. 34) — The Supreme Court holds that although the flag was a federal creation, the States' had the authority to promulgate flag desecration laws under their general police power to safeguard public safety and welfare. Halter involved a conviction of two businessmen selling "Stars and Stripes" brand beer with representations of the U.S. flag affixed to the labels. The defendants did not raise any First Amendment claim.

1908	Flag with 46 stars **Oklahoma (November 16, 1907)**
1909	Robert Peary places the flag his wife sewed atop the North Pole. He left fragments of it as he traveled north.
1912	June 24, President Taft signs Executive Order which establishes proportions of the flag and specifies arrangement and orientation of the stars.
1912	Flag with 48 stars **New Mexico (January 6, 1912), Arizona (February 14, 1912)**
1931	Stromberg v. California (283 U.S. 359) — The Supreme Court finds that a State statute prohibiting the display

	of a "red flag" as a sign of opposition to organized government unconstitutionally infringed on the defendant's First Amendment rights. Stromberg represents the Court's first declaration that "symbolic speech" is protected by the First Amendment.
1942	Federal Flag Code (36 U.S.C. 171 et seq.) — On June 22, 1942, President Roosevelt approves the Federal Flag Code, providing for uniform guidelines for the display and respect shown to the flag. The Flag Code does not prescribe any penalties for non-compliance nor does it include any enforcement provisions, rather it functions simply as a guide for voluntary civilian compliance.

1943 West Virginia Board of Education v. Barnette (319 U.S. 624) — The Supreme Court holds that public school children could not be compelled to salute the U.S. flag. In a now famous passage, Justice Jackson highlighted the importance of freedom of expression under the First Amendment:

Freedom to differ is not limited to things that do not

matter
much. That
would be a
mere
shadow of
freedom.
The test of
its
substance
is the
right to

differ as
to things
that touch
the heart
of the
existing
order. If
there is
any fixed
star in our
constituti

onal
constellat
ion it is
that no
official,
high or
petty, can
prescribe
what shall
be
orthodox

in politics, nationalism, religion or other matters of opinion.

| 1945 | The flag that flew over Pearl Harbor on December 7, 1941, is flown over the White House on August 14, when the Japanese accepted surrender terms. |

1949	August 3 — Truman signs bill requesting the President call for Flag Day (June 14) observance each year by proclamation.
1954	By act of Congress, the words "Under God" are inserted into the Pledge of Allegiance
1959	Flag with 49 stars **Alaska (January 3, 1959)**
1960	Flag with 50 stars **Hawaii (August 21, 1959)**
1962	In the case Engel v. Vitale, the court decides that government-directed prayer in public schools is unconstitutional, a violation of the Establishment Clause. This case is relevant to the

	flag in that it set a precedent for debate over use of the phrase "under God" which was added to the Pledge of Allegiance in 1954.
1963	Flag placed on top of Mount Everest by Barry Bishop.
1968	Adoption of Federal Flag Desecration Law (18 U.S.C. 700 et seq.) — Congress approves the first federal flag desecration law in the wake of a highly publicized Central Park flag burning incident in protest of the Vietnam War. The federal law made it illegal to "knowingly" cast "contempt" upon "any flag of the United States by publicly mutilating, defacing, defiling, burning or trampling upon it." The law defined flag in an expansive manner similar to most States.

1969	July 20 — The American flag is placed on the moon by Neil Armstrong.
1969	Street v. New York (394 U.S. 576) — The Supreme Court holds that New York could not convict a person based on his verbal remarks disparaging the flag. Street was arrested after he learned of the shooting of civil rights leader James Meredith and reacted by burning his own flag and exclaiming to a small crowd that if the government could allow Meredith to be killed, "we don't need no damn flag." The Court avoided deciding whether flag burning was protected by the First Amendment, and instead overturned the conviction based on Street's oral remarks. In Street, the Court

	found there was not a sufficient governmental interest to warrant regulating verbal criticism of the flag.
1974	Smith v. Goguen (415 U.S. 94) — The Supreme Court holds that Massachusetts could not prosecute a person for wearing a small cloth replica of the flag on the seat of his pants based on a State law making it a crime to publicly treat the flag of the United States with "contempt." The Massachusetts statute was held to be unconstitutionally "void for vagueness."
1974	Spence v. Washington (418 U.S. 405) — The Supreme Court holds that the State of Washington could not convict a person for attaching removable tape in the form of

	a peace sign to a flag. The defendant had attached the tape to his flag and draped it outside of his window in protest of the U.S. invasion of Cambodia and the Kent State killings. The Court again found under the First Amendment there was not a sufficient governmental interest to justify regulating this form of symbolic speech. Although not a flag burning case, this represented the first time the Court had clearly stated that protest involving the physical use of the flag should be seen as a form of protected expression under the First Amendment.
1970-1980	Revision of State Flag Desecration Statutes — During this period legislatures in some 20 States narrow the

	scope of their flag desecration laws in an effort to conform to perceived Constitutional restrictions under the Street, Smith, and Spence cases and to more generally parallel the federal law (i.e., focusing more specifically on mutilation and other forms of physical desecration, rather than verbal abuse or commercial or political misuse).
1989	Texas v. Johnson (491 U.S. 397) — The Supreme Court upholds the Texas Court of Criminal appeals finding that Texas law — making it a crime to "desecrate" or otherwise "mistreat" the flag in a way the "actor knows will seriously offend one or more persons" — was unconstitutional as applied. This was the first time the

Supreme Court had directly considered the applicability of the First Amendment to flag burning.

Gregory Johnson, a member of the Revolutionary Communist Party, was arrested during a demonstration outside of the 1984 Republican National Convention in Dallas after he set fire to a flag while protestors chanted "America, the red, white, and blue, we spit on you." In a 5-4 decision authored by Justice Brennan, the Court first found that burning the flag was a form of symbolic speech subject to protection under the First Amendment. The Court also determined that under United States v. O'Brien, 391 U.S. 367 (1968), since the State law was related to the suppression of freedom of expression, the conviction could only be upheld if Texas could demonstrate a "compelling" interest in its law. The Court next found that Texas' asserted interest in "protecting the peace" was not implicated under the facts of the case. Finally, while the Court acknowledged that Texas had a legitimate interest in preserving the flag as a "symbol of national unity," this interest was not sufficiently compelling to justify a "content based" legal restriction (i.e., the law was not based on protecting the physical integrity of the flag in all circumstances, but was designed to protect it from symbolic protest likely to cause offense to others).

1989	Revision of Federal Flag Desecration Statute — Pursuant to the Flag Protection Act of 1989, Congress amends the 1968 federal flag desecration statute in an effort to make it "content neutral" and conform to the Constitutional requirements of Johnson. As a result, the 1989 Act sought to prohibit flag desecration under all circumstances by deleting the statutory requirement that the conduct cast contempt upon the flag and narrowing the definition of the term "flag" so that its meaning was not based on the observation of third parties.
1990	United States v. Eichman (496 U.S. 310) — Passage of the Flag Protection Act results

	in a number of flag burning incidents protesting the new law. The Supreme Court overturned several flag burning convictions brought under the Flag Protection Act of 1989. The Court holds that notwithstanding Congress' effort to adopt a more content neutral law, the federal law continued to be principally aimed at limiting symbolic speech.
1990	Rejection of Constitutional Amendment — Following the Eichman decision, Congress considers and rejects a Constitutional Amendment specifying that "the Congress and the States have the power to prohibit the physical desecration of the flag of the United States." The amendment failed to muster

	the necessary two-thirds Congressional majorities, as it was supported by only a 254 — 177 margin in the House (290 votes were necessary) and a 58 — 42 margin in the Senate (67 votes were necessary).
1995	December 12 — The Flag Desecration Constitutional Amendment is narrowly defeated in the Senate. The Amendment to the Constitution would make burning the flag a punishable crime.
2001	September 11 — The Flag from the World Trade towers survives and becomes a symbol of sacrifice in service, loss, and determination.

2002   June 26 — The 9th U.S. Circuit Court of Appeals in California declares that reciting the Pledge of Allegiance in public schools is unconstitutional because "under God" (inserted into the Pledge in 1954) was a violation of the Establishment Clause, that expression not create the reasonable impression that the government is sponsoring, endorsing, or inhibiting religion generally, or favoring or disfavoring a particular religion. This ruling was reconfirmed in February 2003, and applies only to the 9th Circuit (the following districts: Alaska, Arizona, Central, Eastern, Northern, and Southern California, Hawaii, Idaho, Montana,

	Nevada, Oregon, Eastern and Western Washington, Guam, and Northern Mariana Islands). (See 2010)
2004	June 14 — The Supreme Court declines to hear a case challenging "One nation under God" in the Pledge of Allegiance. "While the court did not address the merits of the case, it is clear that the Pledge of Allegiance and the words 'under God' can continue to be recited by students across America," said Jay Sekulow, chief counsel for the American Center for Law and Justice.
2005	January 25 — Constitutional amendment, sponsored by Rep. Duke Cunningham, introduced. It reads simply, "The Congress shall have power to prohibit the physical

	desecration of the flag of the United States."

June 22 — The Constitutional amendment (see above) is approved by the House (vote of 286-130). It requires Senate approval. Then it must receive approval from 38 states within seven years. |
2006	June 28 — The Senate is one vote short of passing the Constitutional amendment (see above).
2006	July 19 — H.R.42 is passed, preventing condominiums or residential real estate management associations from forbidding the flying of the US flag. Read full law
2010	The 9th U.S. Circuit Court of Appeals in California declares that the phrase "under God" in the Pledge is constitutional.

	The majority decision states, "The Pledge of Allegiance serves to unite our vast nation through the proud recitation of some of the ideals upon which our Republic was founded." It states later, "Coercion to engage in a patriotic activity, like the Pledge of Allegiance, does not run afoul of the Establishment Clause." (See 2002) Read decision [pdf]
????	
	Proposed flag with 51 stars, to be used if a 51st state is added.

Some of the history mine eyes have seen...

- **1565** St. Augustine founded by the Spanish; it is the first European town in the present-day United States
- **1607** Jamestown founded by the English
- **July 4, 1776** Declaration of Independence signed
- **June 21, 1788** Constitution of the United States ratified
- **1803** Louisiana Purchase
- **1861-1865** Civil War

- **1869** Transcontinental Railroad completed
- **1914-1917** World War I
- **1939-1945** World War II
- **1954** *Brown* v. *Board of Education*
- **1965-1975** Vietnam War
- **1989** End of the Cold War
- **1994** North American Free Trade Agreement (NAFTA) took effect

Documents in U.S. History

The documents below are arranged chronologically. They are by no means all the important documents in U.S. history! What other key documents can you think of?

- **Declaration of Independence** July 4, 1776, document declaring the American colonies' independence from Britain and establishing the idea that people have rights that governments may not take away.

- **Constitution of the United States of America** 1788, the fundamental law of the United States, which provides for a government divided into three branches in order to protect the rights of citizens, defend against enemies, and avoid tyranny through a system of checks and balances.

- **Emancipation Proclamation** January 1, 1863, President Abraham Lincoln's directive freeing all slaves in states rebelling against the United States.

- **Thirteenth Amendment** 1865, amendment to the Constitution that abolished slavery.

- **Nineteenth Amendment** 1920, amendment to the Constitution which gave the right to vote to all women 21 years of age and older.

Sources

Eduplace.com/US at a glance
PBS.com
Drexel University/flag history
USHistory.org/flag timeline
47 years of life in America